Helping Out

At the Dog Rescue Centre

Judith Heneghan

WAYLAND

Wayland Australia
Level 17/207 Kent Street
Sydney, NSW 2000

Editor: Louise John
Designer: Robert Walster, Big Blu Design

British Library Cataloguing in Publication Data

Anderson, Judith, 1965-
   At the animal rescue centre. -- (Helping out)
   1. Animal sanctuaries--Juvenile literature. 2. Animal
   rescue--Juvenile literature. 3. Rescue dogs--Juvenile
   literature.
   I. Title II. Series
   636'.0832-dc22

ISBN-13: 9780750264891

Printed in China

Wayland is a division of Hachette Children's Books,
an Hachette UK company. www.hachette.co.uk

Picture acknowledgements:
Photography by Adam Lawrence. Image on page 17
© Shtterstock.

With special thanks to Dogs Trust for all their help
and support.

Dogs Trust is the UK's largest dog welfare charity and
every year cares for around 16,000 stray and abandoned
dogs through a nationwide network of 17 Rehoming
Centres. If you wish to rehome a Dogs Trust dog please
visit our website or call 0207 837 0006. Volunteers are
also an important part of the Dogs Trust team. We have
a wonderful team of full-time dedicated canine carers at
every Rehoming Centre, but with so many dogs to look
after an extra pair of hands is often much appreciated.
Please note that for insurance reasons, volunteers
working with dogs must be 16 or older.

Contents

Saying hello

Today Kiki is visiting the dog rescue centre. He is going to help look after the dogs, and learn about the jobs that people do there. Leslie meets Kiki at the entrance. She is a **canine carer** – someone who takes care of dogs.

Kiki meets Leslie at the dog rescue centre.

Leslie chats to Kiki about the day ahead and explains that dogs often bark when they meet new people. Kiki can hear them barking already!

Leslie says all the canine carers have had lots of training.

KIKI'S DIARY

I'm very excited. Leslie says they don't usually let children help at the centre, but because I'm with my dad I have special permission!

Meeting the dogs

First Leslie takes Kiki to meet some of the dogs. Each dog has a warm, indoor kennel with plenty of space to move around and play, and a cosy bed to sleep on.

Sometimes, two dogs share a kennel, so they have a friend to play with.

Then Leslie takes Kiki outside to the puppy play area. Kiki says hello to two Jack Russell puppies called Peg and Timmy. They are fifteen weeks old, and very lively!

Peg and Timmy are brother and sister.

That's AMAZING!

The rescue centre takes in dogs that have been **abandoned** or **neglected**, and tries to find new homes for them. It looks after 70 dogs at a time.

A new arrival

Max, a ten-year-old Terrier, has just arrived at the rescue centre. His owner wasn't looking after him properly, but the vet says he'll soon be well enough to join the other dogs.

Leslie adds Max's details to the computer.

First, though, Max needs a wash! Kiki and Jane, another canine carer, shampoo his coat, rinse him with water and dry him with a towel. He doesn't seem to mind all the fuss!

Kiki helps to wash Max.

KIKI'S DIARY

Leslie says Max's owners had abandoned him. They probably didn't realise how much training, attention and love a dog needs.

9

Time for a walk

All the dogs need to exercise every day. This helps them to stay healthy, and it's also lots of fun! Leslie and Kiki take six-month-old Trapper for a walk in the field. Trapper loves to sniff out interesting new smells.

The double lead means that Kiki can help to walk Trapper.

Next Kiki helps to exercise a Golden Retriever called Lilly. Lilly is ten. She is very friendly but other dogs make her feel nervous so the **exercise yard** is perfect for her.

That's **AMAZING!**

Dogs enjoy lots of exercise and play. If they don't have toys to chew, people to meet and places to explore they can get bored, just like we do!

Lilly loves jumping over the hurdles.

Daily chores

Lilly is thirsty after her exercise, so Kiki gives her a drink of water. Then he and Leslie go inside to the kitchen. The water and food bowls need washing out. Kiki gets stuck in.

Dogs need plenty of fresh water to drink.

There are lots of bowls to wash.

After washing the dishes, Kiki sweeps the floor while Leslie cleans out some of the kennels. The dogs bark when they see Kiki with the broom. Luckily, he's getting used to all the noise.

KIKI'S DIARY

I didn't mind all the washing up. It was much more fun than doing the dishes at home!

No more muddy paw prints!

Feeding the puppies

Now it is lunchtime. The older dogs are fed in the mornings and evenings but young puppies are still growing so they need an extra meal in the middle of the day. Leslie shows Kiki how to measure out the right amount of food.

That's AMAZING!

Dogs need to eat a carefully **balanced diet**, just like we do. Their special dog food helps to keep their teeth and gums healthy, and their bones strong.

It's important to give each dog the right amount of food for its size.

Then Kiki takes the bowls of food to the puppy area. The puppies Timmy and Peg are excited to see him again. They certainly enjoy eating their food!

The puppies are hungry.

Talking to the vet nurse

Janet is the vet nurse at the rescue centre. She looks after the dogs' health by **vaccinating** them against **diseases** and checking for signs of illness. One of her jobs is to inject a tiny **microchip** under the skin of each new arrival.

Janet shows Kiki the microchipping equipment.

Each microchip has its own number. Once the microchip is in place, the dog can't feel it, but a **scanner** can 'read' it. When Janet knows the number, she can find out who the dog belongs to on a national **database**.

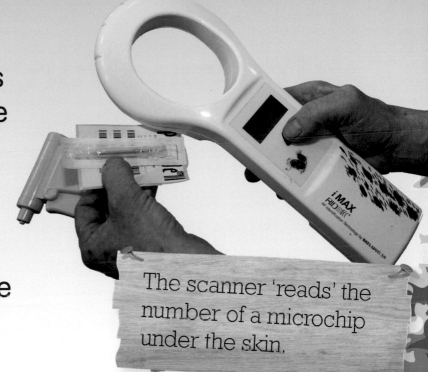

The scanner 'reads' the number of a microchip under the skin.

That's AMAZING!

Lost or stray dogs which have been micro-chipped have a much higher chance of being returned to their owners.

A microchip helps to reunite dogs and owners.

Training fun

Next Leslie and Kiki take Max outside for some training. Dogs need to learn to behave well around people and traffic, so teaching them commands such as 'sit' and 'stay' is very important.

Leslie uses her hand as well as her voice to give the 'sit, stay' command.

Max enjoys all the training challenges.

Leslie shows Kiki how to give the commands clearly and calmly. When Max does as he is told, Leslie rewards him with a treat and lots of praise. Max wags his tail happily. Training is fun!

KIKI'S DIARY

Max did really well at his training session. He even ran along the ramp for me!

Finding a home

A visitor called Emma has arrived in the reception area. She is hoping to find a dog to look after. Kiki takes her to the kennels where she can see the dogs through the glass. She really likes Trapper.

Emma thinks Trapper is the right dog for her.

Kiki gives Emma a form to fill in.

Leslie asks Emma to fill in a form about herself. Each dog is carefully matched with its new owner and Emma needs to show that she will take good care of Trapper.

Time to say goodbye

Kiki's day at the rescue centre is nearly over. 'Do all the dogs find new homes?' he asks. 'Not all of them,' says Leslie. 'But people can **sponsor** one of our dogs, which is another way to care for them.'

It's time to go home.

Kiki says goodbye to Leslie and she thanks him for all his hard work. It has been a tiring day, but he's made some great new friends.

KIKI'S DIARY

Today has been amazing! The puppies were fun and I loved taking Trapper for a walk. I'm really glad he's found a new home.

Kiki with Trapper.

Glossary

Abandoned left behind and no longer wanted

Balanced diet eating lots of different and healthy foods

Canine carer a person who looks after dogs

Database a programme for storing information on a computer

Disease an unhealthy condition or illness

Exercise yard an enclosed area where one dog can play safely

Microchip a small electronic chip that is put underneath a dog's skin so it can be scanned and returned to its owner

Neglected not very well looked after

Scanner a machine for looking inside the body

Sponsor to give money to help out

Vaccinating to inject medicine to protect against disease

Index

Helping Out

Contents of titles in the series:

WAYLAND